T0025334

The Nordic Book of
RUNES

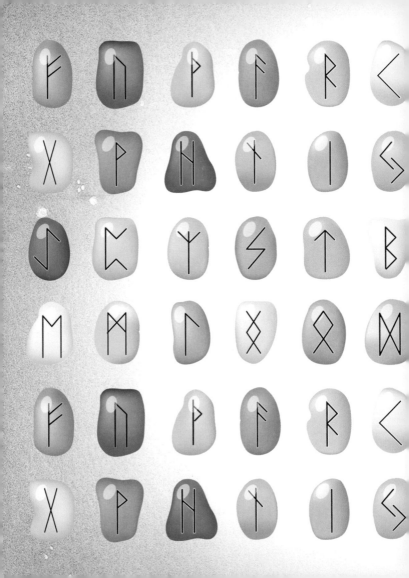

The Nordic Book of
RUNES

Learn to use this ancient code for insight, direction, and divination

JONATHAN DEE

CICO BOOKS

LONDON NEW YORK

This edition published in 2021 by CICO Books
an imprint of Ryland Peters & Small Ltd

20–21 Jockey's Fields   341 E 116th St
London WC1R 4BW   New York, NY 10029

www.rylandpeters.com

1 0 9 8 7 6

First published in 2006 as *Rune Wisdom*

Text © Jonathan Dee 2006 (pages 76–77 and 88–93 © Kirsten Riddle 2015)
Design and illustration © CICO Books 2006, 2021

ISBN: 978-1-78249-744-8

Printed in China

Editor: Liz Dean
Commissioning editor:
Kristine Pidkameny
Senior editor: Carmel Edmonds
Senior designer: Emily Breen
Art director: Sally Powell
Head of production:
Patricia Harrington
Publishing manager: Penny Craig
Publisher: Cindy Richards

CONTENTS

INTRODUCTION
WHAT ARE RUNES?

Runes are angular symbols, usually carved on stone, metal,
or wood, that were made by the ancient Germanic peoples,
the ancestors of the modern Germans, English, Frisians,
and Scandinavians. These diverse races share a common
heritage and once spoke closely related languages. It is not
surprising, then, that they also shared an "alphabetical" tradition
of making meaningful, enduring marks to commemorate
important events, people, and beliefs.

The word "rune," or runa, comes from the language of the ancient
Goths (300–600 CE) and literally means "secret" or "hidden"; this,
in turn, ultimately derives from the early Germanic word ru,
meaning, "mystery." In modern German, raunen also comes from
this root and means "to whisper." Intricately carved runic stones
can be found from the British Isles to Iceland, Germany, Norway,
Denmark, Sweden, Finland, and Russia. There are even some claims
that rune-stones have been found in North America. Many swords
and pieces of jewelry found in the museums of the world are also
inscribed with angular runes. These often display the name of the
object's original owner and, also—and this was most important—
the runic inscription showed that the object was of value, and that
it was imbued with an aura of magical protection.

LEGENDARY MAGIC

From early times, rune-stones were considered to be magical. In around 100 CE, the Roman writer Tacitus described the lives and habits of northern European tribes. As part of his discourse, Tacitus mentioned that in times of trouble or confusion when the gods were to be consulted, the tribal chief would cast nine rune-carved staves onto a white cloth. He would then choose three at random and interpret the future from their symbols. This is the first reference to runes as a method of divination.

Yet, even during the first century CE, the runes were ancient; the earliest examples of runic symbols date from the Bronze Age. These were developed and refined around the second or third centuries BCE, when the northern tribes came into contact with the Mediterranean civilizations of Greece and Rome. However, the Germanic peoples did not believe that the runes were merely the work of man, and considered their origin to be none other than divinely inspired.

The ancient legends and sagas of the North recount the deeds of gods and heroes, but also within these imaginative tales are accounts of the magical origins of these potent symbols. The ninth-century Icelandic narrative poem The Havamal, meaning "The Song of the High One," relates the spiritual journey of Odin, king of the Norse gods who, wounded by his own spear, hangs himself upon the world tree Yggdrasil for nine days and nine nights to gain the secrets of the runes:

Wounded I hung on a wind-swept gallows

For nine long nights, pierced by a spear,

Pledged to Odin, offered myself to myself.

The wisest know not from whence spring

The roots of that ancient tree.

They gave me no bread,

They gave me no mead,

I looked down;

With a loud cry I took up the runes;

From that tree I fell.

The knowledge that Odin gained through his suffering was much more than the ability to write. The runes were believed to contain a potent magical force, to hold within their symbols the secrets of creation and of time itself. To speak the name of a rune or to carve it upon an object was believed to summon an aspect of the power of the universe.

THE ELDER FUTHARK

The runic alphabet is known as a Futhark. This is because just as our word alphabet is derived from the names of the first two letters, alpha and beta, the Futhark expresses the initials of the first six symbols in the runic sequence—Fehu, Uruz, Thurisaz, Ansuz, Raido, and Kaunaz: F, U, T, A, R, K.

Of course the eventual separation of peoples caused variations in runic sets to evolve over a period of time, resulting in sequences such as the Anglo-Saxon and Northumbrian runes. However, the oldest, most complete and established sequence of the runic alphabet is the Elder Futhark. It comprises twenty-four runes in the order shown opposite, and is usually divided into three groups of eight, or "aetts": Frey's aett (see pages 18–35), Hagal's aett (see pages 36–53), and Tyr's aett (see pages 54–73).

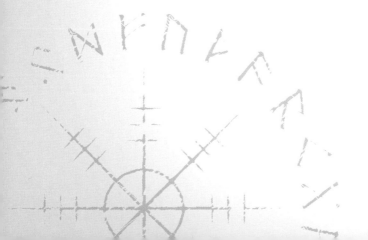

WYRD, THE BLANK RUNE

In modern times, a new rune has been added to
the sequence, bringing the total to twenty-five.
This new rune is represented as a blank stone. It
has been given the name Wyrd, and in a reading
it expresses the concept of fate.

RUNE SYMBOLISM

In the charts on pages 12–15, you will see each
rune's names and its variations, the letter of the
alphabet it corresponds with, its symbolic meaning
in divination, and its calendar association, or "moons" of the ancient
Norse calendar. When you come to do a rune-reading, the calendar
associations can help you to time events—twelve of the runes
relate to the Norse moons, so whenever these appear in a reading,
they can help you to establishwhen a series of events occurred, or
might happen in the future.

Although the runes were formulated long ago, these enigmatic
symbols possess a timeless wisdom. Used correctly, and always
with respect, the runes will reveal the secrets of hidden things,
that which is unknown in the past and present. And, if we are
fortunate, we will see the shape of things to come.

		Rune Name and Variations	Runic Letter and Pronunciation
	1	Fehu, Feoh, Fe	F
	2	Uruz, Ur	U
	3	Thurisaz, Thorn, Thurs	Th
	4	Ansuz, Oss, Os	A
	5	Raido, Raid, Reid, Rad	R
	6	Kaunaz, Cen, Ken, Kaun	K
	7	Gebo, Gyfu, Ge	G
	8	Wunjo, Wynn	W
	9	Hagalaz, Hagall, Haegl	H
	10	Nauthiz, Nyd, Naudr, Naud	N
	11	Isa, Is, Iss	I
	12	Jera, Jer, Ar	J or Y
	13	Eihwaz, Eoh	Long E

Symbolic Meanings	Calendar Associations
Prosperity, beginnings, cattle	September; Wood Moon
Irresistible force, ferocity	February; Horn Moon
Boundaries	-
Divine inspiration, the gods, speech	-
Time, journeys, honor	April, Cuckoo Moon
Passion, insight, inspiration	-
Gifts, generosity	-
Happy endings	-
Disruption, hail and sleet	Halloween and November; Wolf Moon
Necessity	-
Danger, ice	January; Snow Moon
Celebration, endings and beginnings	Midwinter, Yule, and August; Harvest Moon
Progress, adaptability	-

		Rune Name and Variations	Runic Letter and Pronunciation
	14	Pertho, Peoro, Pe	P
	15	Algiz, Eolh, Secg	Z
	16	Sowelo, Sol, Sigil	S
	17	Tiwaz, Teiwaz, Tyr, Tiw	T
	18	Berkana, Beorc, Bjarkan	B
	19	Eoh, Ehwaz	Short E
	20	Mannaz, Mann, Madr	M
	21	Laguz, Lagu, Logr	L
	22	Inguz, Ing	Ng
	23	Othila, Epel, Ethel	O
	24	Dagaz, Daeg	D
	25	Wyrd	-

Symbolic Meanings	Calendar Associations
Chance	May; Merry Moon
Self-interest, healing	-
Energy, poetic justice, the sun	June; Sun Moon
Binding agreements, commitment	-
Birth, motherhood	March; Mother Moon
Ideas, adventure, the animal world	October; Hunting Moon
Mankind, judgment	-
Spirituality, a safe haven, water	-
Health, fertility, creativity, potential	-
Authority, responsibility, inheritance, loyalty	November; Fog Moon
Beginnings and endings, breakthrough, light	Midsummer, July; Hay Moon
Fate	-

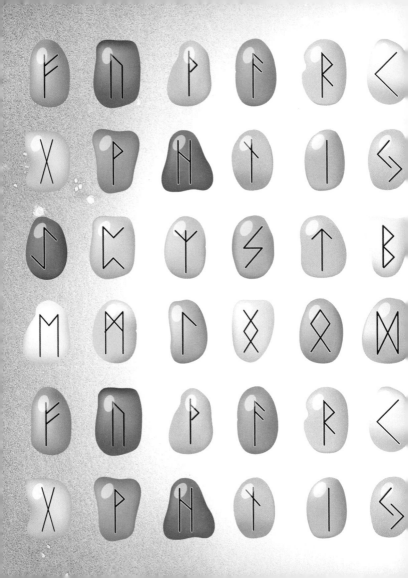

CHAPTER I

THE MEANING OF
THE RUNES

THE RUNES OF
FREY'S AETT

1 FEHU
The rune of prosperity and beginnings

2 URUZ
The rune of irresistible force

5 RAIDO
The rune of time

6 KAUNAZ
The rune of passion and insight

3 THURISAZ
The rune of boundaries

4 ANSUZ
The rune of the divine

7 GEBO
The rune of generosity

8 WUNJO
The rune of happy endings

1 FEHU

(FE, FEOH)

APPRECIATE YOUR GOOD FORTUNE AND RECEIVE ALL GIFTS WITH GRACE

The rune of prosperity and beginnings: In Norse mythology, Fehu is symbolically connected to one of the primal beings of the universe, the great cow Audhumla. Being the first rune, appropriately enough Fehu is associated with beginnings, so any divination that gives Fehu as an answer shows that a new departure is in the offing and the benefits of such enterprise will enrich you, both emotionally and materially.

Fehu is associated with herds of cattle, and since wealth used to be measured in terms of how many cows a person possessed, this rune is also symbolic of prosperity.

The nature of Fehu is feminine and maternal. Indeed, in some instances it can signify a pregnancy, birth, and fertility in general.

Fehu relates to the month of September, or time of the Wood Moon, in the ancient Norse calendar.

Upright meaning: This rune can indicate a time when money is easy to come by. If your divination places Fehu in the future position, then a very fortunate period of material comfort lies ahead. The rune also emphasizes the importance of managing your resources sensibly. Just as a herd must be protected, so this same principle applies to your life savings, too. This means that if you have suffered a time of poverty and financial anxiety, the appearance of Fehu in your reading shows that soon your fortunes will improve rapidly. You will begin to feel more secure and be able to indulge a taste for the comforts of life.

If you are already prosperous, then it may be that Fehu indicates that if you pay a little more attention to managing your resources, you could increase your wealth even more. It also makes it less likely that you lose out through neglect.

Receive the good news that Fehu brings with grace and humility, and perform a charitable act to thank fate or the gods for your good fortune.

Inverted meaning: An inverted Fehu in your reading warns that something valuable is in danger of being lost. It may show a temporary dip in material fortunes, and can also be interpreted as losing a lover or valued friend. It is possible that there may be a problem with conception.

2 URUZ

(UR)

The rune of irresistible force: Uruz is considered to be a rune of great and primordial power. Commonly called Ur, it is symbolically connected with aurochs, the vast, untameable wild bulls of northern Europe. These mighty beasts, now extinct, were once a real peril to man, and so were greatly feared. Thus this rune is emblematic of powerful, unstoppable force. The Anglo-Saxon Rune Poem describes Uruz as "a wild and fierce beast possessing great horns. It is a beast of courage." The rune's connection with a bull pairs it with the first rune, Fehu, which symbolizes cattle, particularly cows.

The word Ur also resembles Norse words meaning metal ore, inclement weather, and ancient. All these add to the masculine, primal, instinctual nature of this rune.

Uruz is associated with February, or Horn Moon in the Nordic calendar.

Upright meaning: The energy revealed by Uruz is very good news if you have been ill, or have suffered from a lack of vitality. It is considered to be a rune of healing, improving physical strength. The appearance of Uruz in a reading is an assurance that health will be restored.

If physical health is not the issue, the force or Uruz will be felt in another sphere. It is likely that events will follow one another with increasing speed, yet you will be endowed with strength of will, physical energy, and the determination to overcome all obstacles. Your confidence will improve, but take care that this does not develop into arrogance. The power of the bull must be treated with respect. A bull may be goaded into action, but it is very difficult to stop its charge once it has begun, so Uruz also urges absolute certainty that you really want to follow a chosen path.

Inverted meaning: When Uruz is in the inverted position, it is likely that rough times are ahead. The powerful charge of the bull may overwhelm you as you are mauled by events over which you have little or no control. You may have problems with self-assertion, or be forced to admit defeat in the face of insurmountable odds. A lifestyle review may be in order, as troublesome health issues are a distinct possibility now.

3 THURISAZ
(THORN, THURS)

KNOW WHERE AND WHEN
YOU MUST STOP

The rune of boundaries: The third rune, Thurisaz, is symbolic of a thorn, the plant world's emblem of sharp defense. By extension, the rune is associated with anything that pierces; therefore, it suggests a serpent's fang or the point of a blade. The word "Thurs" survives today in the name of Thursday, which derives from the name of the great Norse thunder-god, Thor. In turn, Thor himself was a physical giant, considered to be the archetypal giant-slayer, so Thurisaz is described in the rune poems as the "giant's rune". It has been suggested that the very shape of the rune represents the famous hammer of Thor; others suggest that it represents a single thorn on a plant stem. The Anglo-Saxon Rune-Poem has this to say: "The thorn is most sharp, an evil thing to take a grip on, extremely grim for any man who rests amongst them."

Upright meaning: The thorny nature of this rune stone suggests boundaries, because thorn bushes often divided parcels of land. So the appearance of Thurisaz in a reading is associated with personal boundaries, and has come to represent limitations and the perils of "crossing the line". As Thurisaz also brings to mind a fang or a blade, this rune can represent a time of personal danger.

It may warn that there are people around you who are dishonest, or who are actively working towards your downfall. This is particularly the case if your question involves any kind of business dealing. In short, the appearance of Thurisaz in a reading acts as a timely warning, urging vigilance and advises against taking unnecessary risks. Equally, be prepared to defend yourself.

Inverted meaning: Danger is always present when Thurisaz appears in a reading, but this is powerfully emphasized when the rune is in the inverted position. The danger is likely to be greater and more obvious; enemies seem more malicious and determined, and the risk of loss more pressing. It may be that that your own actions are to blame for this situation, with rash decisions contributing to your peril. If so, stop immediately. Assess your situation, and only then proceed very cautiously indeed.

4 ANSUZ

(OSS, OS)

EXPRESS YOURSELF THROUGH THOUGHT AND SPEECH

The rune of the divine: Ansuz is considered to be the rune of divine inspiration. It is associated with the power of speech, the ability to express in words our thoughts and needs. Throughout history, this ability has been considered proof of the divine spark in humanity, a trait that separated us from the animal kingdom and which we shared with the gods themselves. Ansuz is therefore symbolic of thought, words, and sudden flashes of insight.

Upright meaning: Often, the appearance of Ansuz in a reading indicates the sudden development of an entirely new set of circumstances. It is likely that a particular situation will change very swiftly, and you may be at a loss about how to deal with the resulting issues that arise.

However, although your conscious mind may be in confusion, your unconscious mind knows exactly what to do as spirit guides, angels or, as the ancient Norse believed, the "All-Father" Odin himself, will guide you. However you interpret this spiritual intervention, an inspirational power will communicate their understanding to your conscious mind. Answers are likely to come in the form of meaningful dreams or as a set of strange coincidences of the type best described as synchronicity. Of course, Ansuz may express itself more directly as you receive valuable advice from an older, wiser individual, or alternatively your own wit and insight helps you to surmount a problem.

Inverted meaning: Ansuz in the inverted position indicates losing the ability to communicate. This may be interpreted quite literally as an illness affecting the throat, such as losing your voice due to an attack of laryngitis, but it is more likely to predict a situation in which you have difficulty making yourself heard, or in which your views are ignored completely.

Because Ansuz has such a powerful connection with words, it provides a clear warning against speaking out of turn or being indiscrete. Equally, the rune advises that you must take extra care to safeguard important documents, because they are likely to go astray.

The inverted rune also indicates there may be problems with people of an older generation, and delays when traveling.

5 RAIDO

(RAID, REID, RAD)

THE YEAR TURNS AND LIFE
GATHERS SPEED

The rune of time: Raido is associated with time and the rotation of the heavens, which was thought to be like a great cartwheel, eternally revolving. Thus it developed a secondary set of associations, with transport and wheeled vehicles in particular. The word *raido* means "riding," so it is easy to see that when Raido is present in a reading, journeys of all kinds are highlighted.

Raido relates to the month of April, or Cuckoo Moon, in the Nordic calendar.

Upright meaning: Although the road you travel may be bumpy at times, Raido tells you that the journey is worth the effort. If you conduct yourself honorably, doing the right thing by those you meet along the way, you will benefit greatly—not just materially but intangibly, by winning the respect and admiration of all whom you encounter.

If one of your hopes seems to have stalled, the appearance of Raido is very good news showing that things will move forward again very soon. Official and legal affairs benefit too, with all disputes being resolved to your satisfaction.

This is not really a rune of advice, since the message of Raido is that the only judgment you should rely upon is your own; be assured that in general you are on the right track. However, the rune also implies that you should play your cards close to your chest rather than share your confidences with anyone.

Inverted meaning: The literal interpretation of inverted Raido is car problems, or problems with travel in general. However, the reversed rune is likely to refer to deeper issues. Your plans are likely to be disrupted, but don't be disheartened or abandon your long-term aims. The road of life is very rough at the moment and short-term problems may be pressing, so it is very important that you do not lose sight of the bigger picture— keep in mind your ultimate aim and refuse to waver from your course. Carry on, even if you feel that adhering to cherished principles may be spoiling your prospects or making you seem foolish to others. You may be delayed by needless objections or by difficult, complex circumstances, but don't give up. In the end, your actions will be justified.

6 KAUNAZ

(CEN, KEN, KAUN)

LOVE TOUCHES YOU AT A SOUL LEVEL
AND THERE IS SUDDEN CLARITY

The rune of passion and insight: Kaunaz is regarded as the rune of enlightenment. Symbolically, it is connected to a bright, steady flame, as of a candle or torch. It can be likened to beacon fires, which in ancient times were used to pass messages over great distances. Therefore the basic meaning of Kaunaz is the receiving and passing on of knowledge. However, the knowledge represented by this rune has little to do with anything that could be learned in a book, and everything to do with the lessons that life teaches us.

Upright meaning: You may experience the illumination of Kaunaz in the form of a sudden insight, a powerful realization that changes your perspective entirely. This clarity of vision will lead you toward a far deeper understanding of your life, your role, and your aims. The fact that Kaunaz represents a flame means that it also symbolizes the igniting of passion. However, you may become passionate in more ways than one. You could feel very passionate about a person or an ideal, and when Kaunaz makes its presence felt, often the two become strangely mixed up together. It may indicate the beginning of an intense love affair, but it also implies that this special experience will go well beyond physical intensity. Its ultimate effect could be to teach both of you a great deal about yourselves, each other, and the ways of the world in general. There is a sense that everything is progressing as it should; destiny has taken a hand, and you are protected from all harm.

Inverted meaning: When Kaunaz is in the inverted position in a reading, the illumination signified by its upright position is reversed and the light fades.

In love, inverted Kaunaz means that affection is fading. You must let go of the past and be prepared to move on. A more philosophical attitude is to be encouraged. Remember, your personal story isn't over yet, and you can still rely on those lessons you have learned in the past. It is now time for a reassessment. Where do you want to go from here? The answer to that question will convince you that there is wisdom to be gained, even when the outlook appears bleak.

7 GEBO

(GYFU, GE)

CHARITY AND AFFECTION REIGN AS
TWO PEOPLE BOND IN FRIENDSHIP
AND MUTUAL RESPECT

The rune of generosity: Gebo is symbolically associated with contracts and affection, so perhaps it is not so surprising that we use the symbol of this rune as xs to represent kisses. Of course, in former days when most of the population was unable to read or write, documents were often signed with an "x" to represent the personal mark of the signatory.

Gebo represents gifts, generosity, and willingness to help. Like Wunjo, the next rune in the sequence (see page 34), Gebo symbolizes love, but in this case, love of a universal, rather than a purely personal, nature; the rune emphasizes humanitarianism and charitable impulses rather than intimate romantic love. To demonstrate these special values, the Anglo-Saxon Rune Poem sings the praise of the rune Gebo as follows: "Gyfu brings credit and honor which support one's dignity, it furnishes help and subsistence to all broken men, devoid of aught else."

The symbol of the rune Gebo resembles our modern letter "x," and therefore it has no inverted interpretation—its symbol stays the same in both the upright and inverted positions.

Meaning: Gebo's literal interpretation as a gift reveals you may receive a heartfelt present from someone special, such as a lover, a family member, or a friend. It can equally signify a God-given gift, such as an innate talent, ability, or simply a stroke of good fortune. When Gebo turns up in a reading, luck comes as a result of another person's generosity.

This rune may also ask you to examine your readiness to give to those in need. When this rune is prominent in a reading it is highly possible that you will be obliged to help a person or a cause. It stresses the importance of recognizing your personal limitations when judging how much you should give in terms of energy, time, and material resources, and questions what you might require in return, if anything. You should also consider carefully whether any gifts you do give are appropriate to the situation.

Gebo urges a certain amount of caution, because if you are too generous in your giving you may create a state of reliance in the person you wish to help. However, if you are too mean your reputation may suffer, and you could end up feeling guilty.

8 WUNJO
(WYNN)

A KINDLY INFLUENCE ENSURES THAT EVERYTHING WILL TURN OUT WELL

The rune of happy endings: Wunjo is always an encouraging omen in a rune-reading. This is the rune of romance, fun, amorous dalliance, an active social life and, most importantly of all, it is the rune of happy endings. The Anglo-Saxon Rune Poem has this to say about Wunjo: "He lives well who knows not suffering, sorrow nor anxiety, and has prosperity and happiness and good enough house."

Wunjo is also associated with the number three, so be aware that this number may have special significance for you whenever this rune appears. It can also relate to the timescale of events predicted in a reading—three days or three weeks, for example.

Upright meaning: The arrival of this rune cannot fail to lift your spirits, because it denotes a period of spectacular good fortune. This may be found in the home as domestic harmony, or as security in the company of good, trusted friends. However, it is in the realm of romance that the full power of Wunjo is truly expressed, so its appearance can foretell falling in love, and possibly a meeting with someone who is very attractive. This is because Wunjo has strong associations with exceptional physical beauty. If Wunjo appears as an answer in a rune-reading then you can be sure that romance will blossom, a relationship will flourish and a deep contentment will be found.

Wunjo can also show pleasant and advantageous dealings with others. In business, partnerships will be profitable and in your social life, new lasting friendships will be formed.

In health issues, tender loving care will pay dividends, and as Wunjo is also the rune of happy endings, all will be well.

Inverted meaning: Wunjo inverted warns that you are likely to idealize a prospective lover, but the object of your passion is unlikely to be all that they seem. In business there is the danger of underhand dealings, and those you consider friends may deceive you, more to protect your feelings than because they harbor malicious intent.

If inverted Wunjo appears as an answer to a specific question, rather than general guidance or prediction, tradition states that you should wait three days before making any decisions at all.

THE RUNES OF
HAGAL'S AETT

9 HAGALAZ
The rune of disruption

10 NAUTHIZ
The rune of necessity

13 EIHWAZ
The rune of progress

14 PERTHO
The rune of chance

11 ISA
The rune of danger

12 JERA
The rune of celebration

15 ALGIZ
The rune of self-interest

16 SOWELO
The rune of the sun

9 HAGALAZ

(HAGALL, HAEGL)

YOU ENDURE POWERLESSNESS AND UNCERTAINTY WITH PATIENCE

The rune of disruption: Hagalaz is a rune that was once dreaded, and while this is an extreme interpretation, it certainly evokes discomfort in a rune-reading. Considered to be the rune of troubles, Hagalaz indicates disquiet and anxiety. Symbolically it is associated with bad weather, with hailstorms and blizzards. The Icelandic Rune Poem has this to say: "Hagall is cold grain and driving sleet and the sickness a serpent brings." So when Hagalaz appears, plans are disrupted.

As the ninth rune in the sequence, Hagalaz can reveal a time period. It can therefore relate to nine days, nine weeks, or a date with a nine in it. Alternatively, it may point to a date around Halloween time, or during the Wolf Moon in the month of November.

Upright meaning: When taken literally, Hagalaz can indicate a postponement or cancellation of plans because of foul weather. However, like the other runes, its message is more subtle and has a deeper intent. It is likely that the cold winds of harsh reality are about to blow through your life. This is a pitiless, elemental force that cannot be resisted. All you can realistically do at this difficult time is wrap up warmly and take shelter from the storm.

Unfortunately, while you are in confinement in this powerless position, it is too easy for your imagination to run riot and become prone to unfounded fears. It is not surprising, therefore, that Hagalaz is also symbolically linked to the festival of Halloween.

Some interpretations of this rune emphasize its link to gambling. It may show a readiness to risk too much in uncertain times. You can be sure that the odds are stacked against you, but there is still a chance—just a chance—that you will end up a winner if only you sit tight.

Inverted meaning: Hagalaz is an unfortunate rune in any reading, but when it is the inverted position, the ills that it foretells have more to do with lack of forethought, bad planning, misplaced optimism, and badly-timed actions than being victimized by external forces. Caution is vital when Hagalaz is in the reversed position. Its message is to think things through one more time: don't be impulsive, and don't gamble on a long shot.

10 NAUTHIZ

(NYD, NAUDR, NAUD)

NAUTHIZ INCREASES YOUR CHANCES
OF SUCCESS IN THE FACE OF
OUTRAGEOUS FORTUNE

The rune of necessity: Nauthiz expresses the concept of necessity.
The sound of its variant names, Nyd, Naudr, and Naud, suggest
the word "need." Nauthiz is described in the Anglo-Saxon
Rune Poem as "Being oppressive to the heart yet often proves
a help and is the salvation of the children of men who heed it
in time."

Nauthiz therefore suggests a timely warning and strongly
suggests that a dose of reality is about to be injected into your
life. Real life can be harsh, so often a little luck can help us cope.
The shape of the rune may be related to the custom of crossing
one's fingers and hoping for the best.

Upright Meaning: When Nauthiz is found in a rune-reading it
suggests that you need a push in the right direction. It also makes

plain that what must be, will be; taking a philosophical attitude will help you to accept the inevitable.

Nauthiz is likely to make its presence felt when you are anxious and filled with doubt. Feelings of personal security seem to be a distant memory, and your self-confidence may have been severely undermined. A relationship or a cherished project may have failed, and the future seems uncertain. Nevertheless, you can get through this difficult time by showing strength of character.

Nauthiz often shows an unpleasant, unnerving revelation, yet it will turn out to be a positive, character-building experience. This may be a painful time, but in hindsight it will prove to be a turning point. There is also the suggestion of help from family and friends who will encourage the view that although this period is difficult, it is not the end of the world.

Inverted Meaning: When the rune of necessity is in the inverted position, then this is a message from the runes that a veil is cast over the future. It may mean that you are not yet in the right mental or emotional state to accept what the runes have to say. The only thing that seems sure just now is that you are confused and do not know which way to turn.

All that you can do under these circumstances is to be very cautious and watchful. Be patient while you wait for this time of confusion to pass.

11 ISA

(ISS, IS)

ISA, LIKE TREACHEROUS ICE, WARNS OF MIS-STEP AND INJURY

The rune of danger: As its name implies, Isa is the rune of ice and cold. In its shape it resembles an icicle, so it is appropriate that it also relates to the month of January, which the ancient Norse people poetically called the Snow Moon.

In the Anglo-Saxon Rune Poem, the beauty of ice is praised: "It glistens like glass, and is most like a jewel." The symbolism of Isa extends beyond a single icicle, representing snow and ice in all its forms. Perhaps the most descriptive comparison is with great prehistoric glaciers, carving out the forms of the Norwegian fjords with infinite slowness. The states of cold and numbness are also closely linked with this rune.

Isa may also stand for the number seven in a rune-reading, and therefore can express a time period of seven, such as seven days, seven weeks, seven months, or even seven years.

Meaning: When Isa is prominent in a rune-reading, patience not only becomes a virtue, but a necessity. It is true that the power of this rune is unstoppable, just like a glacier; unfortunately, it also possesses the glacier's lack of speed. If Isa appears as an answer to a specific question, the answer will tend to be affirmative— note that there is no inverted meaning for this rune—but events will take their own sweet time. This could be worrying, especially if the question involves a relationship. After all, this is the rune of ice and cold-heartedness, so a cooling of affection and lessening of communication are likely interpretations.

Isa also chills fellowship and cools optimism. Social and business relationships will go through an icy phase, as high expectations seem to come to nothing. It may be that although you and others have been patient, patience is now beginning to wear thin.

Although Isa predicts an uncomfortable, emotionally chilly time, the inevitable delays and frustrations could well be blessings in disguise because your desires will slowly evolve over this period. Isa can also show a respite from emotional turmoil. The true lesson of this cold rune is to tread carefully and surely across treacherous ground. Haste will only lead to more frustration and even worse, you might lose your footing, slip, and fall.

12 JERA

(JER, AR)

A TIME OF JOY AFTER
WORTHWHILE EFFORT

The rune of celebration: After the trials and tribulations indicated by the previous three runes—Hagalaz, Nauthiz, and Isa—it is something of a relief to reach Jera, the rune of celebration. The Anglo-Saxon Rune Poem rejoices with the words: "Jera is a joy to men when gods make the earth to bring forth shining fruits for rich and poor alike."

Symbolically, Jera relates to times of celebration: the end of August, when crops are gathered—the Harvest Moon—and to Christmas, which the ancient Norse celebrated as Yule. This is also the time of the winter solstice, the shortest day of the year in the Northern hemisphere. At this turning point of the yearly cycle, the sun finds new strength. As the days get longer there is the promise of renewal, the spring thaw, and the restoration of fertility. So although Jera represents the most dismal part of the year, it also encourages goodwill, optimism, and warmth of feeling.

Meaning: On a personal level, the appearance of Jera in a reading is an excellent omen because it suggests that you're approaching a major turning point in your life. The impact of this is that any misfortunes that you have recently endured will begin to fade. Soon, you'll be able to breathe a deep sigh of relief, relegate any unpleasant memories to the past, and begin anew.

Joyful Jera can be interpreted as the successful completion of a project, and possibly the signing of a contract that will prove extremely lucrative for you. Equally, this rune can indicate moving into a new home.

The appearance of Jera is good news, and you will feel the emotional mix of excitement along with a frisson of nervousness as you anticipate new and worthwhile things coming into your life. A related interpretation of this rune also connects Jera with harvest time, and its appearance can show you reaping the rewards of your efforts in the past.

Jera has no inverted meaning, so the message of this rune is always positive. As an indicator of time, it is likely to show a period of twelve months before you can celebrate your well-earned success. Also, it can literally point to the Christmas period or harvest as times of particular enjoyment and achievement.

13 EIHWAZ

(EOH)

WITH COURAGE AND PLANNING, THE FUTURE CAN GROW FROM THE REMAINS OF THE PAST

The rune of progress: The symbolic meaning of this rune relates to hunting with a bow. The Icelandic Rune Poem describes Eihwaz as "Bent bow and brittle iron and giant of the arrow."

Eihwaz is also associated with the yew tree, because it is from the wood of this tree that hunting bows were once made. In Norse mythology, Ullr the hunter lived in the valley of the yews. Ullr was the dark aspect of the supreme god Odin during winter, the archetypal wild hunter who is found in the mythology of many countries.

Meaning: Eihwaz is the rune of progress, so in a reading it means that situations are definitely moving on. Even if the pace of your life is slow, with very little seemingly accomplished, a new situation will soon manifest and events around you will move at such a pace that it may be difficult to keep up. The problem will be monitoring developments, so you will need to concentrate and prioritize.

As Eihwaz is associated with hunting, its advice is that you must act like an archer. Be calm, wait until your target is in sight, and at just the right moment loose your arrow. Do not fear that you will miss your chance or your target. Don't be concerned that your quarry might escape. It will not happen, because when this rune appears in your reading you can be sure that you have all the necessary skills, acumen, and shrewdness to hit your mark. Consequently, the Eihwaz often shows that the time has come to gather your courage and be ready to take a risk. It is considered to be an excellent rune for gamblers and for those who live by their wits.

Occasionally, Eihwaz might represent a person, and often the positive, firm influence of a strong-willed, decisive woman. She is likely to be healthy and athletic with a keen interest in outdoor life and sports.

Eihwaz shows that your ability to adapt to changing circumstances and to make fast decisions will be put to the test. However, this is an optimistic rune—it has no inverted meaning —and it promises that excellent opportunities are within your grasp if you are bold. If you are worried about something that is coming up in your life, Eihwaz indicates that expected problems will not arise.

14 PERTHO

(PEORO, PE)

LIFE IS A GAMBLE

The rune of chance: Although both Hagalaz and Eihwaz have a symbolic relationship with games of chance (see pages 38 and 46), Pertho is the supreme rune of gamblers. The word *pertho* means "pawn" or "gaming-piece" in Norse. In fact, one poor sixteenth-century Icelander was convicted of heresy and burned at the stake for having Pertho inscribed on his dice cup, presumably to add to his luck. This is strangely appropriate, because Pertho governs chance, and so has a particular relationship with life's winners and losers.

Pertho is related to the month of May, or the time of the Merry Moon in the ancient Nordic calendar.

Upright meaning: If Pertho is the first or the only rune in your reading, this is a strict instruction from the universe to stop your reading at once—or at least for today. Its appearance in the first position or as a solo stone means that you are not ready to know the answers to your questions at this time. If Pertho appears in the middle or at the end of a reading then the runes will be very responsive, and fate is more kindly disposed towards you. In fact, in either one of these positions, Pertho forecasts a likely celebration.

When the rune is found in the upright position, taking a chance is likely to pay off in a big way. Pertho suggests that you are playing the game of life well, and a winning streak is likely.

Pertho implies secret knowledge, too, so play your cards close to your chest; be discrete, rather than risk revealing your hand too soon.

On a metaphysical note, the rune is also associated with prophecy, so you may soon have psychic dreams that will serve as guidance for the future.

Inverted meaning: If the inverted Pertho is the only rune in your reading or it is the first rune you lay down in a spread, stop and read no more today. If inverted Pertho is found as part of a reading, this is bad news. Fate can deliver a crushing blow when the rune is in this position and losses may be likely if you take any chances.

Pertho is the rune of gambling and now the odds are against you, so take no risks; it is better to miss an opportunity than risk ruin. Any doubts you may have are well justified.

15 ALGIZ

(EOLH, SECG)

LET YOUR SELF-REGARD BE
POWERFUL MAGIC

The rune of self-interest Algiz is a rune that is intimately connected with magical power. Traditionally, it was worn as a charm by those in need of healing and protection. Its power was considered to be so great that it was said not only to protect its possessor but also his family, friends, and property.

In many ways, Algiz can be seen as the rune of self-interest. Its appearance shows that selfishness is not a sin; it is an indicator that at this time, you must put yourself first. Other people's concerns, no matter how important they seem, must be relegated for a while. There may well be a pressing, practical reason for this, such as an illness or a general feeling of mental exhaustion due to the constant and excessive demands of other people.

Upright meaning: Algiz can indicate that it's time to dedicate time to yourself, perhaps by following a personal interest. You may take up a new, fascinating hobby, and expand your horizons to take in new interests and ideas. On a similar note, Algiz can reveal a period of meditation or point the way toward personal enlightenment, adding depth and perspective to your life.

Another aspect of Algiz concerns willpower. If you are embarking on a difficult task, Algiz reassures you that you will have the resolve to carry it through. This is particularly true in the case of a health issue. If you are giving up smoking, for example, you will find the willpower necessary to end the addiction.

Inverted meaning: When inverted, Algiz reinforces the message of the upright position—that it's time to put yourself first. It also predicts that events will speed up. You really need to concern yourself with your own welfare just now, because other people, be they partner, friends, or family, are less sensitive to your needs than usual. Those around you may be completely oblivious to any difficulties that you are experiencing. As a result, you may find yourself in a rather vulnerable situation, liable to be browbeaten into compliance by those close to you. The answer at this time is to seek solitude, and give yourself some space for recuperation.

16 SOWELO

(SOL, SIGIL)

THE URGE TO DEVELOP AND GROW
IS A PATHWAY TO VICTORY

The rune of the sun: Sowelo is the rune of the sun, expressing the life-giving brightness, glory, and good fortune associated with our parent star. The shape of the rune also resembles a flash of lightning, symbolizing personal illumination and, on a literal level, its association with the sun suggests an enjoyable holiday to come. The rune is also said to indicate victory in athletic events and sports. The Anglo-Saxon Rune Poem describes this bright rune as follows: "Sol is the shield of the sky and shining rays and destroyer of ice."

Sowelo relates to the month of June, or Sun Moon in Norse mythology.

Meaning: The appearance of Sowelo in a reading casts a warm glow through a person's fate. It is traditionally said that this rune can undo much of the harm of even the most negative rune-reading.

It is a rune of hope, promising that even in the blackest of circumstances light will again come, and that bad times do not last forever. Thus, Sowelo is an excellent rune to draw when you are in trouble, because a happy outcome is certain. If there is a major decision to be made, Sowelo will cast a beam of light on the situation, banishing all confusion and making the issues absolutely clear.

This is particularly relevant to legal affairs, as Sowelo is symbolically connected to the virtue of justice. So whenever this rune appears in a reading, you can always be sure that the right action will be taken, the correct decisions made, and a fair judgment given. If you are one of the litigants, then it is extremely likely that this fair verdict will go in your favor.

Sowelo is intimately linked with the workings of the human heart. It is considered a good omen for your love life, adding warmth and affection and banishing coldness and hard attitudes. When considering matters of love, Sowelo predicts a long and happy partnership and, if found together with Wunjo (see page 34), marriage is very likely indeed.

Above all, Sowelo signifies a time of happiness and harmony. True love will flourish, and justice will be done. Its wisdom is found in the principle of fair play and contented partnership.

Sowelo has no inverted meaning, so its message is crystal clear.

THE RUNES OF
TYR'S AETT

17 TIWAZ
The rune of commitment

18 BERKANA
The rune of birth

21 LAGUZ
The rune of water

22 INGUZ
The rune of potential

19 EOH
The rune of ideas

20 MANNAZ
The rune of mankind

23 OTHILA
The rune of authority

24 DAGAZ
The rune of light

17 TIWAZ

(TEIWAZ, TYR, TIW)

HONOR YOUR COMMITMENTS
TO ENJOY A LASTING BOND

The rune of commitment: Named after the Norse god of war and justice, the appearance of Tiwaz in a reading suggests conflict of some type, but it also indicates a struggle that is just and necessary. In symbolism it is linked to Polaris, the North Star. The Anglo-Saxon Rune Poem speaks of the rune in these terms: "Tiw is a guiding star, well does it keep faith, it is ever on course over the mists of night and never fails."

Tiwaz is the rune of promises and vows. These are not to be made lightly because anything indicated by this rune is of a firm and unbreakable nature. A bond once made cannot be broken without serious consequences. The most obvious example is taking wedding vows, so this aspect of the meaning of Tiwaz is thought to signify the lasting bonds of love.

Upright meaning: Tiwaz is a masculine rune, indicated by its phallic shape, so the contracts it signifies tends to favor men rather than women. If you are a woman and receive Tiwaz as a response to a relationship question, it gives an extremely passionate answer. It suggests that a strong and handsome man will love you fiercely. Your sex life should be good, but the dangers of jealousy and domination are ever-present. You may also have to sacrifice something valuable in your life to ensure that your link to this man remains unbroken.

Tiwaz also indicates that legal disputes will be resolved favorably. In more physical activities, such as athletics and other sports, Tiwaz bestows victory.

The message of Tiwaz is to hold onto a sense of conviction. As long as you believe in your heart that what you are doing is right, you will have the strength of purpose to succeed in your endeavors.

Inverted Meaning: The inverted interpretation of Tiwaz inclines towards underhanded actions, selfishness, dishonorable motives, and you or another turning their backs on personal responsibility.

Also, the rune in this position can warn of a particular danger for women, because it implies betrayal by a man. It may indicate a relationship that shows all the signs of being lasting, but is in reality a sham. Beware!

18 BERKANA

(BEORC, BJARKAN)

NOW IS THE TIME FOR REGENERATION,
CLOSENESS, AND HEALING

The rune of birth: Berkana has a feminine nature, and is concerned with matters that traditionally were the province of women: intuition, emotions, the arts of herbalism, and healing in the widest sense. Above all, Berkana can be described as the rune of birth. It is symbolically associated with infancy and maternal feelings.

In rune tradition, Berkana is also linked with the birch tree, which was used in springtime fertility festivals. A birch branch was also once hung outside a dwelling to indicate that a woman was in labor there, a symbol of birth associated with midwives and wise women that has been passed down the centuries as the witch's broom.

Berkana is associated with the month of March, or Mother Moon in Norse mythology.

Upright meaning: Berkana may be taken quite literally as the arrival of a new baby or, in a more symbolic sense, as a new beginning, good news, fertility, and times of family rejoicing. It is in this sense that Berkana can be said to indicate a new project that will need care and attention in its early stages to ensure its development, much as a human infant needs the constant love of its mother.

In health matters, Berkana symbolizes the natural regenerative powers of the body and indicates the return of self-confidence that comes with physical recovery. The rune relates to women's issues, too, and is particularly associated with the reproductive cycle. Berkana is a very good omen in a rune-reading if a question of childbirth or fertility is the object of enquiry.

Berkana also brings marriage and nurturing partnerships, signifying enduring emotions. It is likely that the woman will take the lead in this partnership, providing immovable support and loyalty to the man in her life.

Inverted meaning: Berkana in the inverted position often indicates disturbing family news, possibly concerning the health of a relative. A planned celebration may be cancelled. Alternatively, it can show that you may have made a false start, embarking on a course that will lead you nowhere. In this case, begin again. Also, there may be problems concerning conception.

19 EOH (EHWAZ)

IDEAS AND EFFORT ARE REWARDED AS YOU JOURNEY WITH A SPECIAL PARTNER

The rune of ideas: In rune tradition, Eoh represents a proud stallion or a pair of horses who work as a team. The Anglo-Saxon Rune Poem extols the virtues of the rune in these words: "Eoh is a joy to princes in the presence of warriors, a steed in the pride of its hooves, when rich men discuss it, and it is ever a comfort to the restless." Two horses facing each other give this rune its "M" shape.

Eoh is associated with October, or the Hunting Moon in Norse mythology.

Upright meaning: This is the rune of big ideas, major projects, and exciting adventures. Eoh often indicates travel, a shift to a new and fascinating location that will provide lots of mental and physical stimulation. The rune can also indicate moving home, and more congenial surroundings that are in tune with your personality and needs.

Symbolically Eoh represents a team of horses, so in some cases the rune suggests a partnership with someone as strong-willed as yourself. Harnessed together and in step with your partner, great things can be accomplished—greater, in fact, than either of you could possibly accomplish alone. Mutual respect, loyalty, and common goals are also features of this progressive rune. You can be sure that the bond between the two of you will remain strong, even though you will have to overcome many challenges together.

Eoh often has a connection with higher education and urges you toward greater effort, especially if you are involved in research, the sciences, and other investigative fields.

The pace of life is bound to speed up when Eoh appears in a reading. You can be sure of your progress, and your circumstances will improve dramatically. You should also get all the help and advice you need.

Inverted meaning: Problems while traveling or with vehicles are the most common interpretation of inverted Eoh. It can also mean that you are out of step with those around you, or that you or others lack understanding or respect. You may commit to a course of action due to the misjudgment of a partner, who did not see fit to consult you on the matter. Inverted Eoh may also signify health problems for pets.

20 MANNAZ

(MANN, MADR)

THINK THROUGH A PROBLEM BEFORE TAKING ANY ACTION

The rune of mankind: Mannaz symbolically represents mankind, in much the same way that Ansuz, the fourth rune in the sequence, represents the realm of the gods. However, although this rune's meaning may at first appear universal or impersonal, when Mannaz appears in a reading its meaning is, conversely, always personal; it speaks directly to you, the rune-reader, and asks that you carefully consider its message.

This cautious rune is an appeal to your conscience—it urges self-questioning around issues of perfection and achievement, which may also trigger a much-needed reality check.

Upright meaning: When this rune arrives in a reading it is time for reassessment, to question yourself and the motives and aims of those around you. Mannaz urges you to remember that you are mortal, and therefore cannot be perfect. It asks you to be aware of your flaws, but not to let them paralyze you. If you are concerned about your status and the way in which others perceive you, the appearance of Mannaz suggests that you watch out for delusion. Examine which are the real issues at stake, and which may be illusory. Healthy skepticism is your best ally now, so this is not an occasion on which you should commit to any binding agreements—at least until you have given yourself a final opportunity to think everything through just one more time.

Mannaz asks that you resist being pushed along by events, and that you take back some control—so slow down, examine the issues from all angles, then act according to your best and well-considered judgment.

Inverted meaning: When in the inverted position, Mannaz is an ominous rune and provides a warning that an enemy is near. You are well advised to take care of yourself, because someone close by is envious and may even bear you ill will. To deal with this situation you will need courage, but unfortunately the inverted Mannaz also hints at timidity or a lack of readiness to face up to confrontation. The best defence, therefore, is preparation—build up your confidence and arm yourself with arguments to defeat your foe when he makes his move.

21 LAGUZ

(LAGU, LOGR)

ENJOY THE SOFT SENSIBILITIES OF HARMONY, AFFECTION, AND SAFETY IN THE ARMS OF LOVED ONES

The rune of water: Laguz is the rune of water, of the vast expanse of the sea, fjords, safe inlets, and harbors. The Anglo-Saxon Rune Poem is precise regarding the rune's watery symbolism: "Logr is the welling stream and broad geyser and the land of fish." Laguz could easily be a grim rune representing the cruel sea, the "cold, gray widow-maker" of the Norse sagas, but its meaning is opposite. To a seafaring race such as the Vikings, Laguz was a good omen, signifying homecoming, a joyful celebration and a reunion with loved ones. Thus Laguz came to be known as a rune of love, and indeed this rune is a good sign if your question concerns affairs of the heart. The wisdom of Laguz reveals that your love life is now safe from the stormy turbulence of unfettered emotions, and you will find a safe haven in the arms of the one you love.

Upright meaning: Materially speaking, Laguz is another rune that signifies prosperity and success, but it does caution patience. Remember that just as the sea experiences the ebb and flow of the tides, in human life there too is a time and a season for everything. All you have to do is be as calm and imperturbable as the still surface of a lake, and everything will flow to you.

Sometimes you may find yourself in an emotional void with very little going on, when others seem to be making all the moves—leaving you feeling isolated and left on the sidelines as an observer of events rather than actively participating. If this is the case, the appearance of Laguz in a rune-reading is an excellent omen because it advises patience. It informs you that you don't have to do anything special to change your situation, but rather that the situation will change around you. A fair wind will blow in your direction very soon, indicating that your time will surely come.

Inverted meaning: The seas of emotion are overly turbulent when Laguz is inverted. It may be that you are being too assertive and demanding of attention, or too impatient or aggressive. You may feel hard done by, and curse fate for your misfortunes. Try to be more rational; take deep, slow breaths, and have patience.

22 INGUZ
(ING)

The rune of potential: Inguz is a rune possessed of great potential, and it is symbolically connected to health, well-being, and fertility, particularly for men.

As a rune of new beginnings, it often indicates great originality and fertility of mind, and shows that reserves of energy are available for new projects and ideas. With no inverted meaning, the message of Inguz is always positive.

Meaning: The appearance of this rune in a reading is good news for those who are seeking a new, more fulfilling job. However, to discover a new start that really changes your life, old business must be completed first. You may have to make a conscious decision to close a door on one phase of your life entirely. If this is the case, you will soon find within you the courage and determination to conclude old business and make the right decisions to move on, even if just now it all seems far too complicated to tackle.

Although these periods in life are often fraught with great anxiety and concern for the future, the true wisdom of Inguz is not to worry because the rune promises that there will be plenty of opportunities to replace that which has gone with something better.

In some ways, Inguz can be regarded as the rune of no regrets. There is very little point in crying over past actions and events, but given time, this rune will prove that you will gain far more in the future, which will be more precious than anything you have lost.

Another aspect of Inguz is problem-solving, so if you have been vexed by a trying situation that has defied your best efforts and taken up a tremendous amount of time and attention, the good news is that the solution is now very close to hand. It may be that you are simply too close to the issue. Try ignoring the matter for a while; give yourself a little space. You haven't yet seen the whole picture, but when you do, you'll realize that the answer is obvious and far more straightforward than you had at first imagined.

On a similar theme, Inguz can be regarded as a signal to book a well-earned vacation, or simply take a day or two off work to refresh your flagging spirits and regain a much-needed sense of perspective.

23 OTHILA

(EPEL, ETHEL)

LOYALTY, RESPECT, AND IDENTITY ARE THE FOUNDATIONS OF FAMILY

The rune of authority and responsibility: Othila is associated with the clan, the family, and the nation. It represents patriotism, family loyalty, and proper respect for authority, law, established customs, hallowed tradition, and devotion to a cause or religious path. Othila is therefore intimately connected with questions of identity.

The rune also represents something that stands the test of time. A set of values that is rarely questioned may seem to be staid and dated, yet is somehow strangely comforting. The Anglo-Saxon Rune Poem refers to the rune meaning as a continuity of tradition within the family: "Epel is dear to all men, they may enjoy there at home whatever is right and proper in continual prosperity."

Othila is associated with the month of November, or Fog Moon in the ancient Norse calendar.

Upright meaning: The rune is often present in a reading to suggest dynastic concerns, indicating a time when traditions become more valuable in life. Engagements, marriages, and births are one aspect of this, while dealing with wills and family property is another. In some cases the rune may signify an inheritance, but this need not be anything material. In fact, it is more likely to be expressed in the characteristics you share with your ancestors and relatives.

You may need to take advice from older people or from experienced professionals and, in addition you are likely to find that you are asking yourself "What would this person have done in this situation?" By the time the influence of Othila is over, you will have moved closer to your heritage and origins.

Inverted meaning: Quarrels about money and status are often shown when Othila is in the inverted position. Disputes may arise, involving inheritance or insurance claims. There is certainly disloyalty and an attempt to overturn established principles; some kind of loss may be indicated, possibly due to theft or even legal trickery.

In some cases, the inverted Othila warns that care must be taken to avoid accidents with machinery. Be cautious; don't be too impulsive or take unnecessary risks.

24 DAGAZ

(DAEG)

THE RUNE OF MIDSUMMER ILLUMINATES A HIGH POINT IN YOUR LIFE

The rune of the sun: Dagaz represents the sun at noon and the long hours of glorious sunshine at midsummer. In many European languages, Dagaz is related to the word "day," and is the rune of happiness and light. The Anglo-Saxon Rune Poem describes the joy associated with this rune: "Daeg, the glorious light of the sun is sent by the High One, is beloved of men, a source of hope and happiness to rich and poor and a service to all."

Since Dagaz is symbolic of sunlight, it can indicate personal enlightenment, and a wider perspective on life. Many secrets will be revealed when Dagaz arrives. Old mysteries will be explained and people will tend to be more forthcoming—this is because in a symbolic sense, no darkness can remain in the bright glare of sunlight.

Dagaz is associated with midsummer, the month of July, or Hay Moon in the Norse calendar.

Meaning: Dagaz is associated with laughter, fun, and wonderful times. At last an old, frustrating and possibly sad set of circumstances has come to an end and good times beckon. You will be enlivened and ready to put your efforts into a fresh burst of enjoyable activities. Dagaz could signify a breakthrough in a particular matter. This will be greeted with a sigh of relief followed by a sense of great exhilaration as you surge forward in life once more.

The rune is also connected to the idea of playfulness. With so many worries lifted from your shoulders you will feel free to look at the world with child-like wonder and a marvellous sense of fun and humor. In a similar vein, any news concerning children will be both welcome and beneficial.

Dagaz may also relate to future travel. indicating a wonderful, warm, and memorable holiday.

Many rune-readers consider that Dagaz is always auspicious; after all, it has no inverted meaning. However, this should be qualified, because if Dagaz does appear in a negative position in a reading or it repeatedly falls face down, it is likely to mean that the good times symbolized by the rune will be delayed for a while. Even so, you can be sure that an excellent period of enjoyment, freedom from anxiety, and the dawning of great happiness is imminent.

25 WYRD

THE BLANK RUNE

DESTINY IS AT WORK WHEN THE ENIGMATIC BLANK RUNE APPEARS

The rune of fate: The blank rune is a modern addition to the traditional twenty-four rune sequence of the Elder Futhark. Its use is optional, although many experienced rune-readers find it a very useful innovation. It has been named Wyrd after the intricate web of fate woven by the mysterious grey sisters called the Norns. The Icelandic saga *The Voluspa* describes the Norns:

> *Thence come three maidens who much do know;*
> *Three from the hall beneath the tree;*
> *One they named Was, the second Is,*
> *These two fashioned a third, named Shall Be.*
> *They established law,*
> *They selected lives*
> *For the children of time,*
> *And the fates of men.*

The three Norns personified the past, the present, and the future. In Norse mythology, their names are given as Uld, Verdandi, and Skuld. The sagas have it that their web of fate expressed designs of such scope and complexity that if one of the witches was to stand on a mountain top in the furthest east and another waded far out into the depths of the ocean, the full extent of their pattern still could not be seen.

These three prophetic witches survived the Viking age to be remembered in various guises such as the three fairies who bestowed gifts upon Sleeping Beauty, and the Weird Sisters of Shakespeare's play *Macbeth*.

Meaning: The blank rune in your reading reveals the workings of fate. Should it be the only rune, or the first rune in your spread, then stop at once, because you are not ready to receive the answers of the runes today.

If Wyrd should occur in any other position in a rune-reading, you are about to reach a point in life that is completely predestined. You are approaching a period in which your free will will have little influence, and events will progress as they have been ordained.

As an answer to a specific question, the appearance of Wyrd tells you that now is not the right time for a particular project or relationship.

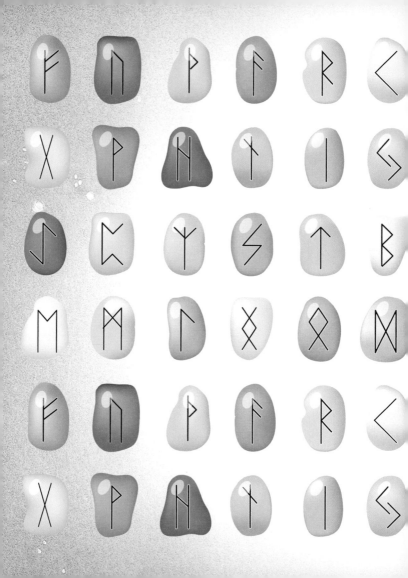

CHAPTER 2

WORKING WITH
RUNES

GETTING STARTED

To begin working with runes, you'll need a set of stones and a rune bag to keep them in. You may wish to invest in a set of pre-made runes: the majority of sets will include the 24 Elder Futhark stones and the blank Wyrd stone, as detailed in this book. However, you may also choose to create your own.

MAKING YOUR OWN RUNES

- Buy blank stones or collect stones that appeal to you. It is best if they are all roughly the same size and shape. You could even use a piece of wood that you then cut into smaller, uniform pieces.
- The symbols can be painted onto the stones or carved into them.
- Consecrate the runes by burying them in the earth or soaking them in fresh water overnight.
- Spend some time getting to know each one, holding the rune stone in your hands and letting any thoughts or images spring to mind.
- Keep your runes safe in a small bag; one made of black silk is ideal to protect the runes from negative energy. Keeping a piece of quartz with the stones will enhance the magical properties of each symbol.

HOW TO LAY OUT RUNES

Before beginning a rune reading, it is important to clear your
mind of everyday thoughts. This process will help you to receive
messages from your rune divination that you or the person you
are reading for easily understands.

Take some deep breaths and become mentally passive as you
shake your rune bag to mix the runes well. Think of a specific
question, or ask for a general overview of your life just now.

READING YOUR OWN RUNES

When reading for yourself it can be difficult to grasp the wisdom
of the runes immediately. One technique is to lay out the runes,
then note their positions and meanings using keywords (see
pages 12–15). Put the runes and notebook away, and get on with
other things to allow your intuition to get to work. Later, lay out
the runes again and read the full meanings; you'll find the spread
easier to interpret.

READING FOR SOMEONE ELSE

When you have randomized the runes sufficiently by shaking the
rune bag, pass the bag to the person you are reading for and
allow the other person to shake and mix up the runes some
more. Now ask the person to think of a question as they shake
the bag.

It is important that this process is never trivialized. It is equally vital that the question asked of the runes is carefully considered, and never flippant. You can be sure that the runes do not give their wisdom to the foolish.

Now take the bag and randomly pick the rune stones one by one, and lay them out in one of the set patterns, or Runic spreads (see pages 80–87).

DRAWING ODIN'S RUNE

It's best to begin by drawing a single rune, known as the Rune of Odin. This is the most common way to begin a rune reading—a single rune is chosen to answer a specific question. It can also be used as a personal horoscope to give a general forecast for the day, or as an aid to meditation. You can also use the Rune of Odin as a preliminary to a more general reading as it will give the background to a question and may bring to light a particular issue which can be more fully explored in subsequent readings. When you have finished interpreting Odin's Rune, replace it in the bag. If you choose to continue, you can either draw another single rune to represent the present or future or choose to lay out a few runes in one of the slightly more complex traditional patterns shown in the following pages.

If you continue rune-readings for a long time, the runes will eventually begin to repeat themselves. This means that the reading is over and you should pack away your runes for the day.

Since the runes never give an answer that is flippant or trivial, Odin's Rune always reveals an important issue affecting your life.

THE RUNES OF THE NORNS

Named after the three goddesses of fate in Norse mythology, each of the three runes is named after Urd, Verdandi, and Skuld, or Past, Present, and Future. Use this spread as a simple way to gain an overview of any situation.

1—PAST   2—PRESENT   3—FUTURE

1. **The Place of Urd—the Past**
   Past events that have a direct relevance to the present situation and the question asked of the runes.

2. **The Place of Verdandi—the Present**
   Present circumstances and choices that can be made in the near future.

3. **The Place of Skuld—the Future**
   The culmination of events that are already known, but which may reveal a twist of fate.

THE RUNIC CROSS

The Runic Cross uses six runes, laid out in the pattern shown below. Use this spread when you need to understand the obstacles in your path, revealed by rune 5, as a way to move forward into the future, symbolized by rune 6.

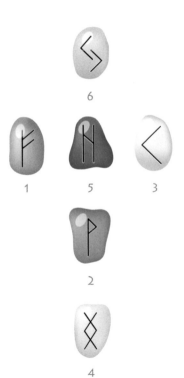

1. The past and its influence upon the present.
2. The present.
3. Hopes and fears—in short, how you envisage the future.
4. The reasons for the question or the matter at issue.
5. Obstacles and possible problems.
6. The eventual outcome.

THE MAGIC SQUARE

This spread of nine runes is an extension of the Runes of the Norns. Use it when you need a detailed reading to help reveal what is hidden—unconscious motivations, desires, and events.

The Magic Square gives eight aspects of your situation, plus a prediction (rune 9). The bottom line of runes reveals the past, the center line the present, and the top line, the future.

Lay out the runes in the order shown opposite, and read them in this order, too.

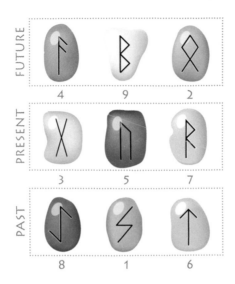

FUTURE

PRESENT

PAST

4 9 2

3 5 7

8 1 6

1. The past and its present influence.
2. Your attitude to the future and general state of mind.
3. Things that are hidden from you yet influence the events in your life.
4. How these hidden influences will affect the outcome of your question.
5. The present circumstances of your life.
6. Your memories and attitudes to events of the past.
7. Your present attitude.
8. Secrets in the past, or hidden influences on past events.
9. The best possible outcome.

THE KEYSTONE READING

This spread reveals the wisdom you may gain from your present situation, and will help inspire you to take action when necessary—carry rune 4 from your reading with you as an amulet of guidance and mediation.

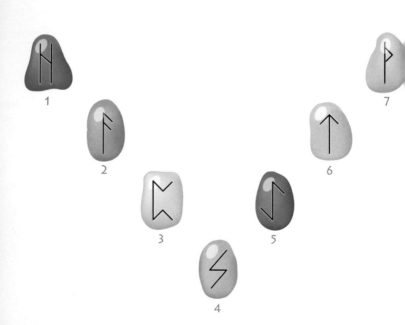

1. The past and its general influence on the present circumstances.
2. The present and more specifically the reason for the reading.
3. The general course of luck and prospects for the future.
4. This is the "keystone", the single most important rune in the reading. It reveals the wisdom of the reading and advises the best course of action that the questioner should take.
5. The outcome and what the questioner has learned from the experience.
6. Problems that may delay or upset the questioner's plans.
7. The outcome.

THE NINE-RUNE CAST

The Nine-rune Cast may be the oldest form of rune divination; the Roman writer, Tacitus, described a similar method in the second century CE. The Nine-rune Cast does not have a formal arrangement, but is led by the intuition of the person consulting the wisdom of the runes.

Place a white cloth the size of a large handkerchief on a flat surface such as a tabletop. Then randomly select nine runes from your rune bag. Hold them in your hands while formulating your question. When you consider the time to be right, and you are in a suitably receptive state, cast the nine runes onto the white cloth from a distance of 6 to 9in (15 to 23cm).

A number of runes will land face upward, while others will be face down. Those runes that have landed at the center of the cloth are the most important, the closest to the issue.

The face-up runes reveal the circumstances that are known to you; read them first. The face-down runes reveal the pattern of the future. Interpret as you go, allowing your intuition to guide you.

The runes at the very edges of the cloth represent background influences, such as other people's opinions. Runes that missed the cloth altogether can be ignored.

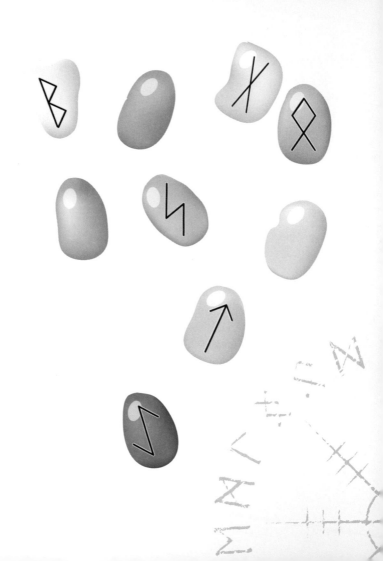

PERSONAL POWER SYMBOLS

As well as working with runes for divination, you may find you have a personal response to one or more of the symbols on the stones. If so, you may wish to make that rune your personal power symbol, something that you connect with on a higher level which could be extremely potent and help in every area of life.

Once you have identified your personal power symbol, you need to give it significance. This book already details the traditional meaning of each runic symbol, so you may want to simply enhance this energy; if you feel it has a different meaning for you, you can create something unique.

As a starting point, hold the chosen rune in front of you. Spend a few minutes focusing on the shape of the symbol. Close your eyes and bring the symbol to mind. Imagine it on a big screen in front of you. Concentrate on the symbol and nothing else. Let any thoughts or feelings float through your mind and continue to focus on the shape. When you are ready, open your eyes and record any thoughts you had. You may have developed a feeling or emotion that you now associate with your symbol. This will give you an idea of the kind of energy with which you are working. For example, if you felt hot and full of vitality, this might mean the symbol is associated with action, strength, and health. On the other hand, you might have felt emotional and loving, which would suggest that the symbol resonates love energy.

WORKING WITH YOUR SYMBOL

It is up to you how you work with your personal power symbol stone, though some suggestions are offered here. The important thing is to do what feels right because this is personal to you.

CHARGING A STONE WITH ENERGY

One of the best ways to charge a rune stone is in a simple circle ritual, which you can perform outside or in. Start by setting out a circle using stones—perhaps your other rune stones—or crystals. The circle is your sacred space where you can raise energy and charge your symbol. Sit in the center of the circle and begin by placing your chosen rune stone on a piece of paper in front of you. If you want, you could choose to light some candles or burn some relaxing oil, such as lavender or geranium essential oils, to create an uplifting atmosphere. Place both hands over the stone and imagine pouring light and love into the symbol. Make a statement of your intention, such as, "I charge this symbol with light and love." To charge the symbol with a specific intention—for example, to give you confidence and assist you with your goals—take the piece of paper and write words that capture the spirit of the energy you would like to raise. You might write "power," "success," and "vitality." Fold up the paper and hold it in both hands. Say, "By the power of the divine, I charge you from this moment in time. My intention set, my goal is clear. I draw this powerful energy near!" If you have lit a candle, you might like to burn the paper in the flame to seal your wish or, if you are performing the ritual outside, you could bury the paper in the earth while repeating the chant.

Once your rune stone is charged with energy, you can carry it with you to draw upon its power whenever needed.

CREATING AN ALTAR

Keep your personal power symbol stone in a special place at home by creating an altar—simply choose a window ledge or coffee table and fill it with items associated with your symbol. Include items that reflect the four elements of earth, air, fire, and water. You might have a candle in an associated color to represent fire, a piece of crystal to represent earth, a vase of flowers for water, and a wind chime for air. Place a dish in the center of your altar and, for an extra power boost, surround it with quartz crystal points. Keep the points directed at the dish and place your rune inside it overnight to charge it.

If you prefer, you might want to have a special box where you store your personal power symbol stone. Again, it is up to you what you put in the box. You can use it for personal wishes and requests associated with your stone.

BODY ART

Some people like a more personal relationship with their symbol and choose to have it tattooed upon their skin. This is not necessary to make a connection, but if you do want an extra power boost, try drawing it upon your skin with an ink pen that you can wash off later. There are various points upon the body, including the chakras—small energy centers—that are ideal for placing your symbol. Here is a brief guide.

Wrists: Easily accessible, wrists are the perfect choice for placing your symbol. A nerve center that calms the heart rate, imagine the symbol penetrating deeply beneath the skin as you draw.

Picture white light flowing around your body, increasing energy levels and general vitality.

Palms: The center of the palms radiates energy. If you rub your hands together for a minute and then pull them apart, you will feel the magnetic pull of that energy between your palms. Placing a symbol on your palms will increase health and vitality and stimulate healing power. Imagine swirling balls of light in each hand as you draw your symbol. To reflect power and confidence, place your hands over your heart and picture yourself in a cocoon of golden light. To help friends or family who need healing, hold your hands out in front of you and imagine sending light and love in their direction.

Throat: The throat chakra, situated at the front of the lower part of the neck, governs self-expression and creativity. It is the chakra that can help you speak your truth. Although you might not want to draw your symbol with ink here, you can wear it as a pendant over the throat chakra to activate this energy or simply trace the symbol with your fingers. Turquoise is the color most associated with this chakra, so if you can combine this shade with your symbol, you will enhance its effectiveness.

Chest: The heart chakra is situated just above the center of the chest. It governs love and emotions as well as self-healing. If you want to increase the flow of love into your life or you just need to balance your emotions, trace your symbol in this space. For added effect, instead of using ink, use a little rose water, which also increases the love vibration.

Stomach: Just above the belly button, you will find the sacral chakra. This energy spot governs intuition and can help you develop psychic skills and tune into positive energy. It also helps boost self-esteem when activated. If you need to increase your confidence, radiate happiness, or just improve your intuition, this is the place to draw your personal power symbol. Orange is the color most often associated with this chakra, so you could use orange ink or henna to enhance the effects.

Soles: The soles of your feet are important energy centers. They connect with the earth and help to anchor you in times of trouble. If you are looking for balance and strength, try tracing your power symbol on each sole. Once you have done this, stand barefoot, either inside or out, and imagine roots growing from each sole and extending deeply underground. Drop your weight down to your lower legs and feel the roots keeping you strong and secure. If you have an important meeting to attend or you are going on a journey, draw your symbol on both feet to help you walk tall and speak with confidence.

INDEX

PICTURE CREDITS